Sight Word Tales™

little   has

Little Bo-Peep's Lost-and-Found Sheep

by Jane Quinn
illustrated by Kelly Kennedy

SCHOLASTIC INC.

New York • Toronto • London • Auckland • Sydney
Mexico City • New Delhi • Hong Kong • Buenos Aires

Designed by Maria Lilja
ISBN-13: 978-0-545-01672-8 • ISBN-10: 0-545-01672-X
Copyright © 2008 by Scholastic Inc.
All rights reserved. Printed in China.

First printing, January 2008

12 11 10 9 8 7 6 5 4 3 2 1   8 9 10 11 12 13/0

Little Bo-Peep **has** lost 15 sheep.
Poor **little** lass! She must **find** them all fast!

She **finds** one with a spoon on the run.

She **finds** two in a very big shoe.

Little Bo-Peep **has found** three of her sheep!
But the **little** lass must **find** the rest fast.

She **finds** six on a wall made of bricks.

Little Bo-Peep **has found** nine of her sheep!
But the **little** lass must **find** the rest fast.

She **finds** three in a tub on the sea.

Little Bo-Peep **has found** 12 of her sheep!
But the **little** lass must **find** the rest fast.

She **finds** three more doing a chore.

Little Bo-Peep **has found** all 15 sheep!
She **has found** every one!
Time for a **little** fun.

The **little** lass sneaks away
to hide in some hay.

She **found** us, but we can't **find** her!

Now all of the sheep must **find Little** Bo-Peep!

Sight Word Review

Do you know the four sight words in this book? Read aloud the word on each sheep.

find   found

little   has   find

has   found   little

14

Sight Word Fill-ins

little   has
find   found

Listen to the sentences. Then choose a sight word from the box to fill in each blank.

Word Box   **little**   **has**   **find**   **found**

1 My sister _____ not come home yet.

2 Ladybugs are very _____.

3 They cannot _____ their mittens.

4 He _____ five dollars on the ground.

5 May I have a _____ more milk?

6 She _____ blue eyes.

7 Last week, we _____ a frog in the woods.

8 Where did you _____ that book?

Answers: 1. has 2. little 3. find 4. found 5. little 6. has 7. found 8. find

Sight Word Cheers

Celebrate the new sight words you learned by saying these four short cheers.

L-i-t-t-l-e! Give a yell!
What do these six letters spell?
A sight word that we all know well —
Little, little, little!

H-a-s! Give a yell!
What do these three letters spell?
A sight word that we all know well —
Has, has, has!

F-i-n-d! Give a yell!
What do these four letters spell?
A sight word that we all know well —
Find, find, find!

F-o-u-n-d! Give a yell!
What do these five letters spell?
A sight word that we all know well —
Found, found, found!